275

D1215373

ENGLISH ROMANESQUE SCULPTURE

1066-1140

ENGLISH ROMANESQUE SCULPTURE

1066-1140

by

GEORGE ZARNECKI

PH.D., M.A.

1951

ALEC TIRANTI LTD.
72, CHARLOTTE STREET,
LONDON, W.1

CONTENTS

Made and printed in the United Kingdom.

I

INTRODUCTION

And Historical Outline

THE scope of this little book is limited to a short period in the history of Romanesque sculpture in England from the Norman Conquest to the years immediately following the death of Henry I in 1135. Although we know that Norman influences were felt in England for a decade or two earlier, the year of the Conquest provides a useful, conventional date with which to mark the beginnings of Anglo-Norman art. The choice of 1140 as the end of the period to be considered demands an explanation. Nothing of any historical or artistic consequence occurred in that year. It was, however, about that time that the first important regional school of sculpture in England came to an end. About that time, also, English sculpture was developing considerable stylistic changes; during the reign of the Conqueror and of William Rufus Anglo-Norman sculpture was in its infancy; the thirty-five peaceful and prosperous years of Henry I's rule were a period of experiment, expansion and consolidation. By 1140 or thereabouts full maturity had been reached.

It is incorrect to call the sculpture of this period *Norman* because such a term entirely excludes the English element in that sculpture. Actually, the correct term is *Anglo-Norman* and this should be used to distinguish Romanesque sculpture in England from that of the Continent. Anglo-Norman sculpture is part of a wider artistic movement embracing the whole

71915

of western and central Europe and is a regional development of that style.

By Romanesque art in its widest sense we understand the art that followed the late antique period and lasted until the Gothic : the vital period of transition from classical to fully developed medieval art. In a narrower sense it is the art of the eleventh and twelfth centuries, and it is only with art of this period that we are concerned here.

It is usually claimed that the introduction of Norman Romanesque art into England resulted not from any logical artistic development but from the political consequences of the Battle of Hastings. It should be remembered, however, that the art of the late pre-Conquest period in England had numerous links with Normandy and that there was even then a peaceful exchange of artistic ideas across the Channel. The pro-Norman sympathies of Edward the Confessor are well known, and it is firmly established that his great foundation, Westminster Abbey (consecrated in 1065), was modelled on Jumièges Abbey in Normandy.

But the sculpture of the late pre-Conquest period seems to have been little, if at all, affected by Normandy. There was, of course, no uniform style of pre-Conquest sculpture in England. Scandinavian-derived elements were predominant in the northern and eastern parts of the country, where the Viking traditions were strongest; in the south, centred in Wessex, the so-called "Winchester Style" was widely adopted. This latter highly sophisticated sculpture of purely English inspiration was very different from any contemporary sculpture in Normandy.

It has recently been established that following the

reform of monasticism in Normandy carried out by William of Volpiano, Abbot of Saint-Benigne at Dijon who was called to Normandy by Duke Richard II in 1002, Norman sculpture of the eleventh century was strongly influenced by Dijon. The best evidence of this relationship is the Abbey of Bernay with its important series of carved capitals. Curiously enough, while there is strong architectural evidence of the influence of Dijon on pre-Conquest England (Wulfric's rotunda at St. Augustine's Abbey, Canterbury) there are no signs of similar sources for English sculpture. Such elements in late eleventh and early twelfth century English sculpture as have their origin in Dijon came to England not directly, but, by way of Normandy.

One might hazard a guess that even without the political conquest England would eventually have adopted the Norman form of Romanesque art, modified perhaps by influences from other parts of France or even Germany. Not unnaturally, the process of Normanisation became very rapid almost immediately after the Battle of Hastings. It was William the Conqueror's deliberate policy to appoint Normans as bishops and abbots in England and to draft monks from Normandy. Since the English clergy had been active in their support of Harold, William lost no time in replacing them by his own nominees from Normandy. Less than twenty years after the Conquest only one English abbot remained in charge of a monastery.

No sooner had a Norman bishop or abbot taken charge of an English see or monastery (or often both, owing to the peculiar English institution of the cathedral monasteries) than the building of a new church began. Not without reason, the Normans considered Anglo-Saxon church architecture inferior to their own and missed no opportunity of erecting new buildings that in scale even surpassed their Norman models. Soon most of the great churches of England were in this new Anglo-Norman style. The feverish building activity that characterises this early Anglo-Norman period produced such suitable conditions for experiments and improvements that by the end of the eleventh century the Anglo-Norman builders created a monument that must be regarded as a " landmark in the architectural history of western Europe ": Durham Cathedral, the first building to be roofed with ribbed vaulting.

While early Anglo-Norman architecture has been the subject of much careful study for more than a hundred years, the sculpture remains very little known. The preference given to architecture in the study of the English art of the period is understandable. It had by far the greater importance in the subsequent development of European art as a whole. The method of vaulting first applied at Durham, and soon also in some other English churches, spread to Normandy and thence to Ile-de-France where it laid the foundations of Gothic architecture.

It cannot be claimed that English post-Conquest sculpture had any substantial effect on the development of sculpture on the Continent. True, some decorative motives, such as the chevron and, at a slightly later period, the beak-head ornament, spread from England to Normandy and even further afield. But these motives could not produce the revolutionary changes in sculpture that ribbed vaulting achieved in architecture.

Our study is made extremely difficult by the very bad state of preservation of most of the material, by the destruction of a great number of buildings of the period, and by the scarcity of dated sculptures. Moreover, we know practically nothing about the artists: their training, their organisation, their methods of work, what tools they used. Nor do we know what was the relationship between artists and patrons and how far work was dictated or influenced by the patron. We lack any documents that might throw light on such things. All we have are the monuments themselves, and it is from them that we must try to glimpse what we can of the creative spirit that gave them birth, and of the conditions under which their creators worked.

It has not been possible in a book of this length to give anything more than a brief outline of the development of English Romanesque sculpture between 1066 and 1140. But by limiting the scope of the book to a comparatively short period it is possible to examine a number of works that are never included in books of a more general character. Yet even here only a small selection of the relevant material could be discussed and illustrated. For, in spite of destruction by man and time, there is still a wealth of sculptures scattered over the country. They have a simplicity, a sincerity and often a beauty that can be enjoyed even by the most discriminating taste. The purpose of this book is to help in the understanding, appreciation and, above all, in the enjoyment of English Romanesque sculpture. For those who wish to learn more about the period from the best authorities a list of books for further reading is given at the end of the volume.

II

English Sculpture during the Reigns of William the Conqueror and of William Rufus, 1066 - 1100

With a few exceptions, the first churches built after the Conquest were based on Norman models and were, at least in part, obviously erected by Norman masons. No wonder, therefore, that their sculptural decoration such as it is, closely resembles the sculpture of Normandy.

It has been strongly believed that in the field of early Romanesque sculpture Normandy was one of the most backward and barren districts of France and that the Normans never achieved, nor even attempted, more ambitious plastic decorative schemes. More recent research, however, shows that there is a great deal of good sculpture in Normandy, but that it is usually confined to the decoration of capitals. These are mainly of the volute type, sometimes decorated with one or two rows of upright leaves (Diagram 2, page 11) in obvious imitation of the classical Corinthian capitals (Diagram 1). But, beside these comparatively simple examples, there are also some carved with geometrical patterns, with foliage, with masks, with animals and even with human figures. The decoration of Bernay Abbey is an example of this more sophisticated style of Norman sculpture, dating from the first half of the eleventh century.

Nothing of similar variety and quality can be found

1

Rome, Temple of Vesta.
Corinthian Capital.

2

Bayeux Cathedral, Normandy.
Corinthian-derived Volute Capital.

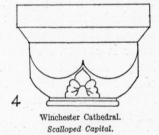

3

Worcester Cathedral.
Cushion Capital.

4

Winchester Cathedral.
Scalloped Capital.

in the earliest Anglo-Norman churches. It is all the
more surprising when architecturally they not only
imitate but even surpass their Norman models in scale
and boldness of construction. The use of wall paint-
ings seems to have been one of the principal means of
decoration; there are numerous proofs that suggest
that even capitals, those architectural members that
are most suitable for sculptural decoration, were

11

covered with painted designs. The modest character of the earliest Anglo-Norman sculptures can be judged by examples at Canterbury and elsewhere.

The only surviving capital enriched with sculpture from Archbishop Lanfranc's cathedral at Canterbury (*c*. 1075) is of the Corinthian-derived type (Fig. 11), that was so common in Normandy. Similar capitals can be found as far apart as in St. John's Chapel, Tower of London (*c*. 1082), Richmond Castle in Yorkshire (*c*. 1071) and Lincoln Cathedral (before 1092). At Durham Castle (*c*. 1072) this form of capital is combined with a simple mask (Fig. 3). In the crypt of Gloucester Cathedral (*c*. 1089) only two capitals are enriched with sculpture : one was to have received a simple foliage design, but it remains unfinished; the other is carved on one side only with a head with a long moustache (Fig. 4). The capitals of the nave piers of Blyth Priory in Nottinghamshire (*c*. 1090) have even more simply carved heads placed between the angle volutes.

Surprisingly, the richest series of early Anglo-Norman sculpture is to be found not in any big cathedral or abbey but in a small chapel in Durham Castle, founded by the Conqueror in 1072 (Fig. 1). The vaulting of this chapel is supported by six slender columns, each crowned by a volute capital enriched with sculpture that combines geometrical pattern, mainly the diaper, with figure motives. Geometrical sculpture was very common in Normandy throughout the Romanesque period and it was under direct Norman influence that it became popular in England.

The Durham capitals (Figs. 3, 5 - 9) are often described as crude and even barbarous. But, judged by their highly decorative effect rather than their naturalism, they certainly are not. Moreover, the sculpture is applied to the capitals with a great understanding of their architectural function, which is to transform the round shape of the columns into the square shape of the abaci. This in particular can be said of the capital carved with four figures at the angles, supporting the abacus (Fig. 9). Here the heads of the figures replace the usual volutes, and the upraised arms suggest the idea of pressure and support. This motive of " supporters " in Romanesque sculpture was ultimately derived from the classical figure of Atlas. Supporters somewhat similar to those at Durham are found on a capital in the crypt of Saint-Benigne at Dijon (early eleventh century) (Fig. 10) and it is quite possible, in view of William of Volpiano's mission in Normandy, that the Durham capital derives from that source by way of Normandy. The late eleventh century capitals in the small church at Bramber in Sussex (Fig. 12) also show a certain connection with Dijon, through Norman channels.

One of the most characteristic features of early Anglo-Norman architecture, and one that throws some light on its formative sources other than those coming from Normandy, is the cubic or more commonly called cushion capital (Diagram 3, page 11). As has been said already, the capitals in use in Normandy before the Conquest were of the volute type (Diagram 2). These were introduced into England by the Normans and the examples mentioned so far are of that type. But the volute capitals are outnumbered in Anglo-Norman buildings by the cushion capitals, which were unknown in Normandy until they were introduced there from England. Cushion capitals had already been used in some Anglo-Saxon buildings and were derived, no doubt, from Germany, where they were quite common from the beginning of the eleventh century. The sudden popularity of cushion capitals in England after the Conquest indicates that the Normans were not totally unfriendly to local achievements, and that once they adopted a feature from Anglo-Saxon buildings they used it widely.

The inclusion of cushion capitals into the Anglo-Norman architectural vocabulary is paralleled later in the eleventh century when, under influences from other regions of France, and also from Germany, there were certain departures from pure Norman models.

The cushion capitals retained their popularity until the end of the twelfth century and they evolved into numerous variants, known as scalloped capitals. These were the result of the multiplication of the semi-circular curves on the sides of the capitals, each carried down to the necking in a semi-cone (Diagram 4, page 11). Throughout the eleventh century the cushion and the scalloped capitals had hardly any carved enrichments, but they seem to have been decorated frequently with painted designs.

Outside the big cathedrals and abbeys and therefore free from the direct influence and control of the Normans, Anglo-Saxon sculpture seems to have been allowed to develop undisturbed. Such carvings as the relief at Newton in Cleveland in Yorshire (Fig. 13) and tympana at Uppington in Shropshire (Fig. 15), Byton in Herefordshire (Fig. 16) and indeed many others, although found in places widely separated, have as a common characteristic the flat relief and well defined outlines that are more closely related to the pre-Conquest technique of cross-carving than to contemporary sculpture of the Anglo-Norman type. The love of the capricious line forming intricate, and often abstract, patterns, so typical of some Anglo-Saxon carvings, survived in many works that date from the late eleventh or early twelfth centuries.

A few sculptures that fall within this period show unmistakable signs of Viking influence, particularly of the Urnes style. There is proof that this type of ornament found favour even with some of the Normans (the crozier of Flambard, Bishop of Durham, is decorated in this style) and it is therefore not surprising that its influence can be traced, though in isolated examples, from Sussex (Christ at Jevington) to Yorkshire (capitals at Kirkburn) (Figs. 17 and 18).

III

English Sculpture between 1100 and 1140

The thirty-five years of Henry I's comparatively peaceful reign were marked by profound changes not only in the political, social and religious but also in the artistic life of the nation. Building was carried on as energetically as in the previous period. A great many churches that were begun earlier were completed, and most of the Anglo-Saxon buildings that had survived the first zeal for rebuilding under the Conqueror (e.g. Lichfield and Peterborough) were now replaced by Anglo-Norman structures. The growing prosperity of the monasteries made necessary the enlargement of even recently built churches and monastic buildings. Lanfranc's cathedral at Canterbury, for instance, built in the seventies of the eleventh century, was enlarged with a new " glorious " choir as a chronicler calls it, that was dedicated in the presence of the King in 1130. Many entirely new churches were started, amongst them Reading Abbey (1121), King Henry's own foundation, in which he was buried in front of the high altar.

But while in the previous period the sculptural decoration of the buildings was very modest, much more elaborate plastic schemes were now gradually introduced. Sculpture was not now restricted to capitals and some tympana, as in the eleventh century. On the exterior of churches carved decorations would frame the doorways and windows and also run along the walls in enriched corbel tables (Fig. 33), string-courses and arcadings (Fig. 34). The doorways often had carved voussoirs, tympana, capitals and shafts (Fig. 77). The corbels excelled in grotesque carvings, while blind arcades consisting of richly carved shafts and intersecting arches often encircled the church. Even the wall surface was sometimes enriched with geometrical patterns such as the lattice diaper or the scale pattern. The interior sculptural decoration of the churches was usually even more extensive. The capitals of piers and responds and of the triforium galleries and the chapels were often profusely carved, and the shafts and the spandrels of the triforium galleries frequently had geometrical enrichments. Some of the church fittings, such as fonts and screens, were also decorated with sculpture. But perhaps the most sumptuous decoration was applied to

16

the cloister arcades. Surviving fragments show carving on both the capitals and the voussoirs forming the arches of the arcades.

It has often been said that this lavish church decoration was initiated by the Cluniac monasteries and that it was in keeping with their love of elaborate liturgy. But the use of sculpture on a scale hitherto unknown appears to have been spontaneous throughout Western Europe. In England, although the urge for this rich architectural sculpture may have come from the Continent, the actual work was done by native artists. In contrast to the previous period when Norman masons were beyond question very often employed, there are no indications that foreign masons were working in England during the reign of Henry I. Reading Abbey is a clear illustration of this point. Although built under the supervision of monks sent from Cluny, its sculpture bears not the slightest trace of Burgundian influence.

The changes in the iconography, or subject-matter, of twelfth century English sculpture are not less striking. It will be remembered that in the eleventh century the choice of subjects was limited to geometrical or foliage motives, to animals and birds, to masks and to occasional human figures. The few religious subjects that exist are comparatively simple and rather late: St. Eustace with a horse and hounds at Durham (*c*. 1072) (Fig. 7) is one notable exception. Nevertheless, even in the last decade of the eleventh century there was one example of sculpture of a definitely narrative character: the capitals in Westminster Hall (Figs. 25 and 26). Narrative or "historiated" capitals became fairly frequent in the twelfth century, although they never attained the popularity they had in France. A few capitals in Hereford Cathedral (*c*. 1115) (Figs. 27 and 28) and Southwell Minster (*c*. 1120) (Figs. 29 and 30) and single examples at Westminster Abbey (*c*. 1120) and Reading Abbey (*c*. 1130) (Fig. 62) are the most important " historiated " capitals in our period.

Of the religious subjects, carved not only on capitals but on other architectural members, those depicting scenes from the life of Christ were naturally by far the most popular. The growing cult of the Virgin, which was to reach its fullest expression in Gothic art, produced a representation in English Romanesque sculpture of the Coronation of the Virgin that can be claimed to be the oldest surviving example of that scene (capital from Reading Abbey, *c*. 1130) (Fig. 62). Even when Old Testament scenes were represented, those were chosen that foreshadowed the events of the New Testament: the Sacrifice of Isaac, for instance (tympanum at Rochester and a capital in Winchester City Museum, probably from Hyde Abbey, both *c*. 1140) as symbolic of the Redemption.

Secular scenes that occur fairly frequently in our period are the Signs of the Zodiac, the animals of the Bestiaries, fighting warriors, riders, *jongleurs,* and a number of scenes that were suggested to the sculptors by contemporary life. But by far the most popular and the most numerous subjects in English Romanesque sculpture, and indeed in Romanesque art as a whole, were those fantastic, chimerical creatures, half human, half animal or bird, against which the puritan of the twelfth century, St. Bernard, protested in vain:

18

" To what purpose are those unclean apes, those fierce lions, those monstrous centaurs, those half-men, those striped tigers, those fighting knights, those hunters winding their horns? Many bodies are there seen under one head, or again, many heads to a single body. Here is a four-footed beast with a serpent's tail ; there, a fish with a beast's head. Here again the forepart of a horse trails half a goat behind it, or a horned beast bears the hinder quarters of a horse. In short, so many and so marvellous are the varieties of diverse shapes on every hand that we are more tempted to read in the marble than in our books, and to spend the whole day in wondering at those things rather than in meditating the law of God. For God's sake, if men are not ashamed of these follies, why at least do they not shrink from the expense?" (*)

But except in the Cistercian order, in which figural art was prohibited, neither expense nor St. Bernard's ridicule prevented such subjects being used.

The iconographical sources of Romanesque sculpture were various. Some motives such as centaurs, syrens and griffins, were obviously taken over from classical art, others were copied from precious oriental silk textiles, and the ivories and metalworks of past ages supplied many other motives. Illuminated manuscripts provided one of the most important sources— their richly decorated pages and initials had a profound influence on stone sculpture.

From a few existing examples from later periods we know that in their work medieval sculptors used pattern-books containing a great variety of designs. It was probably due to the wide circulation, perhaps commercial, of such pattern-books that we find sculptures amazingly similar in subject in places as far apart as Pavia and Canterbury. The mystery plays that were such a popular feature of medieval life also had a great effect on sculpture. An example of the unmistakable influence of an acted scene, of its costumes

* The letter, or " Apologia," to William, Abbot of St. Thierry, from which this extract is taken (in the translation of G. G. Coulton), was written by St. Bernard about 1125.

and of the expressions of the actors, can be seen on the Chichester reliefs (Figs. 80 - 82).

But figural subjects formed only a part of the artistic language of Romanesque sculptors. Foliage and geometrical patterns, which they used with remarkable variety and ingenuity, were equally important to them.

Religious and moral subjects were certainly much rarer in the English sculpture of our period than in the contemporary sculpture of France or Italy. We lacked in particular their great iconographic schemes, which are sometimes displayed in a long series of reliefs, on large doorways, or on a number of related capitals. Of the nine capitals that survive from Reading Abbey, for instance, only two have religious carvings (Figs. 61 and 62): the rest are carved with purely decorative motives. This lack of religious sculpture is indeed striking in the metropolitan cathedral church at Canterbury which was ruled in succession by two such eminent theologians as Archbishops Lanfranc and Anselm. There is not a single religious subject amongst the dozens of capitals in the crypt and on the exterior arcades. English Romanesque sculpture can hardly claim the title of " Poor Man's Bible."

The stylistic characteristics of sculpture between 1100 and 1140 were less uniform than in the eleventh century. This was due to the formation of numerous local workshops, some of which developed very individual styles. In a few cases we can even speak of regional schools. These, however, did not spring up until about 1120. The first two decades of the century were marked by the rapid spread of Anglo-Norman style. By then it had penetrated beyond the big churches, abbeys and castles into the rural districts (Figs. 19 - 24). Between about 1110 and 1115 a geometrical decorative motive that remained one of the most typical features of English Romanesque sculpture throughout the whole Romanesque period, was introduced almost simultaneously in a number of buildings. It was the chevron or zig-zag ornament.

Figural subjects, however, gradually attained greater prominence; and, in addition to the works in which they were combined with geometrical motives (Figs. 19 and 23), there are a number of sculptures in which human figures are used alone (Figs. 24, 27 and 28). Some of these early figural carvings are admirable in their own forceful style (Figs. 27 and 28). The influence of manuscript illumination, to which reference has already been made, is seen in a linear style that derives from drawing. The Southwell Minster capitals (Figs. 29 and 30) are a notable example of this method.

A number of works that survive in Northamptonshire which are very much alike stylistically, lead us to believe that a regional school existed in the district. In this case we are particularly fortunate : one of the works has the date 1124 in the dedicatory inscription. This is at St. Kyneburgha's church at Castor. The series of capitals of the tower arches (Figs. 39, 41 and 42) are carved with decorative motives in low relief. As on the Kirkburn capitals (Figs. 17 and 18) traces of the Viking style survive in some of these carvings but there are also a few figure subjects of a totally different origin; if we compare one of these scenes

21

(Fig. 39) with an illuminated manuscript (Fig. 40) the source of the inspiration is at once clear. One of the capitals is carved with two fighting warriors armed with clubs and shields, with a weeping woman standing behind. A very similar subject is found on a font at Wansford (Fig. 38). The churches at Sutton and Maxey both have capitals that are undoubtedly the product of the same school. The sculptures of this Northamptonshire school of about 1120 combine the Viking traditions with the Anglo-Norman style in a particularly happy way and show great liveliness and a strong decorative sense.

A school of far greater scale and importance existed at the same time further south. It originated at Canterbury during the building of the new choir of the cathedral in about 1120.

The capitals of the crypt beneath the choir (Figs. 47 and 49-57) are among the best works of English Romanesque sculpture. They show a great mastery of technique and are, in one respect, unique in Romanesque sculpture as a whole : in no other case is the influence of locally produced manuscripts on sculpture so plainly evident as at Canterbury. The Canterbury scriptorium flourished throughout the twelfth century and the inspiration of almost every carving can be traced to the books produced there.

The crypt of Canterbury Cathedral was built about 1100 and the capitals used there were of plain cushion type. When some twenty years later they were decorated with sculpture, their original shape was partly obscured by carvings. One Canterbury sculptor, however, applied the sculpture to three of the capitals in such a way that the cushion shape was not

22

only retained but even underlined by sculpture (Fig. 47).

The influence of Canterbury spread rapidly: first, in a modified form to Westminster Abbey and then, almost simultaneously to Reading Abbey and Hyde Abbey, Winchester (both c. 1130). A little later it spread to Romsey Abbey, Christchurch Priory, Rochester Cathedral and to many other places in southern England. An isolated example as far north as Durham (Fig. 60) is the measure of the success of the style originated at Canterbury.

The method of underlining the cushion shape of a capital by sculpture, so brilliantly carried out at Canterbury, was further developed at Reading. At Romsey and Rochester a similar method was used for the decoration of scalloped capitals (Figs. 48 and 70).

The late works of the Southern School bring us beyond the reign of Henry I. While the earlier works of the school were purely decorative and conceived in a flat relief with clearly defined outlines, in the later stages of the school's development the treatment is more plastic. The use of ornamental foliage, so profuse in many earlier works, gave way to figural subjects in high relief and a more monumental style. This is a general tendency in the works of about 1140, with perhaps the exception of eastern England. There, the Viking traditions were still alive and the flat style lived longer. A capital from Norwich Cathedral (Fig. 76), carved with two snake-like dragons, is a tribute to the vitality of these Scandinavian traditions.

And even in such a magnificent work as the Priors' Doorway at Ely Cathedral (Figs. 77 and 78) which, it has been claimed, has certain Italian features, the flat

23

linear style shows that the Viking influence had not been entirely superseded. Certain resemblances between the Priors' Doorway at Ely and some Norwich capitals (Figs. 76 and 79) may perhaps justify us in suggesting the existence of an East Anglian workshop that was responsible for the sculpture at both places. Some capitals in a similar style at Wakerley in Northamptonshire also belong to this group.

Two last works that must be mentioned are two reliefs in Chichester Cathedral (Figs. 80 - 82). These powerful sculptures belonging to the closing years of our period, are works of the highest artistic excellence. But they are unique in the period, there is nothing to explain them, no works that in any way prepare us for the strong dramatic emotion that finds expression in these two works of genius. A small fragment at Toller Fratrum in Dorset showing Mary Magdalen at the feet of Christ is the only other surviving work of this sculptor.

It may be that these masterpieces of deeply religious art can be best understood when seen against the background of the turbulent, unhappy years of the Great Anarchy under King Stephen. The civil wars that followed the death of Henry I certainly did not encourage artistic activity and if, in spite of such lamentable circumstances, the artists persisted in their work, it is proof indeed of the creative force of the age.

DESCRIPTIVE NOTES TO THE PLATES

With one or two exceptions, the illustrations are arranged in chronological order

1. DURHAM CASTLE CHAPEL. *Circa* 1072.
   This is a small chapel supported by six slender columns with carved capitals. These are undoubtedly the richest series of eleventh century capital-carvings in England. Some of them are illustrated in Figs. 3 - 9.

2. ST. JOHN'S CHAPEL, TOWER OF LONDON. *Circa* 1080.
   The only sculptured decoration in the chapel consists of modest enrichments to the capitals. The great majority of them have flat projections in the form of a Tau-cross. Capitals of a similar type are also found in Westminster Abbey, Canterbury Cathedral and Norwich Cathedral.

3. DURHAM CASTLE CHAPEL ; capital. *Circa* 1072.
   The prominent angle volutes and upright leaves springing from the plain necking are of the usual Norman type which is derived from the classical Corinthian capital. The triangular space between the volutes determines the form of the mask and of the leaf with which it is carved.

4. GLOUCESTER CATHEDRAL ; capital in the crypt. *Circa* 1089.
   Similar in shape and decoration to the previous example, but without the upright leaves. The mask is carved as a human head with a long, twisted moustache. Capitals of this type are common in Normandy, e.g. at Mont Saint-Michel. It is significant that the founder of Gloucester Cathedral was Abbot Serlo (1072 - 1103) who was previously a monk at Mont Saint-Michel.

5. DURHAM CASTLE CHAPEL ; capital. *Circa* 1072.
   Two confronted animals with their heads replacing and serving the purpose of angle volutes. There is no attempt to model the bodies of the animals but they are enriched with diagonal incised lines, a method commonly used in eleventh century sculpture in Normandy. The background is carved with a diaper pattern, one of the geometrical ornaments popularised in England by the Normans.

6. DURHAM CASTLE CHAPEL ; capital. *Circa* 1072.
   Snake set on a diapered background.

7. DURHAM CASTLE CHAPEL ; capital. *Circa* 1072.
   This is the only carving in the chapel of Durham Castle with a religious subject. The nimbed figure leading a horse and hounds towards a stag carved on the other side of the capital probably represents St. Eustace. According to the twelfth cen-

tury historian, John of Salisbury, the nobility of his time esteemed hunting and hawking as " the most honorable employments and most excellent virtues." It is most fitting, therefore, to find St. Eustace, the patron saint of huntsmen, carved in the chapel of a feudal castle.

8. DURHAM CASTLE CHAPEL ; capital. *Circa* 1072.

Human mask on a diapered background. The necking of this capital is the only one in the chapel enriched with the twisted or cable pattern, a rare occurrence in the eleventh century. In the second quarter of the twelfth century this decoration became extremely popular throughout the country.

9. DURHAM CASTLE CHAPEL ; capital. *Circa* 1072.

One of the most accomplished in the chapel. Four figures of supporters are placed at the angles, their heads serving as angle volutes and their arms raised as if to carry the abacus and thus also the weight of the vaulting. This motive has its obvious origin in the figure of Atlas of classical art.

10. DIJON, SAINT-BENIGNE ; capital in the crypt. *Early eleventh century.*

The figures of supporters are carved here not at the angles as at Durham (Fig. 9) but on the sides of the capital ; nevertheless the similarity of motive is undeniable. It should be remembered that the reform of monasticism in Normandy was carried out by William of Volpiano, Abbot of Saint-Benigne. The monastic links between Dijon and Normandy quite naturally resulted in certain artistic links. Some of the motives in Norman sculpture that were derived from Dijon were later carried across the Channel and we find them in various parts of England.

11. CANTERBURY CATHEDRAL ; capital in the crypt. *Circa* 1075.

This capital came from the church built by Archbishop Lanfranc and was later re-used when the choir of his church was enlarged. The decoration of the capital consists of the familiar angle volutes and two rows of upright leaves. This capital is closely matched by several examples in the crypt of la Trinité (Abbaye aux Dames) at Caen, founded by Matilda, wife of William the Conqueror, about 1062.

12. BRAMBER (SUSSEX), ST. NICHOLAS' ; capital of the chancel arch. *Late eleventh century.*

This capital provides another example of the artistic connections between England, Normandy and Dijon. It is of the voluted type but with heads replacing the angle volutes proper. The peculiarity of this example is the rectangular projection in the centre of the capital just below its abacus ; this projection is carved with an animal. The earliest example of this type of capital is found at Dijon (Fig. 14), but it is soon followed by its

Norman imitations at Bernay and Caen (la Trinité). Another example of the use in England of this method of decoration is found at Southwell Minster (Figs. 29 and 30). At Bramber the animal spreads on to the capital proper and is biting a bird ; other animals and birds are carved on either side of each angle head. The carving is very flat and the placing of the figures is determined by the shapes of the surfaces they decorate. The subordination of sculpture to architectural shapes is peculiar to early Romanesque sculpture. It was only in the later twelfth century that sculpture freed itself from architectural bonds.

13. NEWTON IN CLEVELAND (YORKSHIRE, NORTH RIDING), ST. OSWALD'S ; carved stone. *Late eleventh century.*

It was found in 1827 in the churchyard and is now built into the tower. It is often referred to as a Saxon carving, but stylistically it is much closer to a group of late eleventh or early twelfth century sculptures, found in all parts of the country and having as a common characteristic very flat relief, left as a plain surface. The subject of the Newton carving is typical of the group—dragon-like animals fighting. In this particular case there are two animals: one a quadruped with open jaws and the other, facing it, a winged dragon with an additional head at the end of its long tail.

14. DIJON, SAINT-BENIGNE ; capital in the crypt. *Early eleventh century.*

The carving of foliage and an animal enclosed by a rectangular frame is placed between the angle volutes. As already noted (Fig. 12) this motive originated at Dijon and came to England by way of Normandy.

15. UPPINGTON (SHROPSHIRE), HOLY TRINITY ; tympanum over the north doorway. *Late eleventh century.*

The carving represents a dragon, with the tail forming a twisting, ornamental pattern. It is similar in execution and spirit to the Newton relief (Fig. 13).

16. BYTON (HEREFORDSHIRE), ST. MARY'S ; tympanum built into the south wall. *Early twelfth century.*

In contrast to the previous example, this tympanum is carved with a religious subject—the Agnus Dei with a cross. This symbol of Christ is enclosed by a medallion flanked by three-stranded looped patterns. The tympanum has certain decorative merits but it is, admittedly, like some previous examples, a naive, rustic piece of work.

17-18. KIRKBURN (YORKSHIRE, EAST RIDING), ST. MARY'S ; capitals of the nave window. *Circa* 1100.

The interlacing ribbon-like pattern decorating these capitals is derived from Viking art, most particularly from the Urnes style;

27

this ornamental style is characterised by intricate, almost abstract interlacing forms. The Kirkburn capitals are some of the very few surviving examples of Urnes-influenced Romanesque sculptures in England.

19. BARTON SEAGRAVE (NORTHAMPTONSHIRE), ST. BOTHOLPH'S ; tympanum over the north doorway. *Circa* 1100.

The tympanum is made up of eight separate pieces of stone joined together in two horizontal rows, a fact that influenced the character of the decoration. Each stone was carved in the mason's lodge before it was put in position and, particularly in the upper row, there is little relation between the carving of one stone and that of its neighbours, each having been carved as an independent unit. A head is carved in the centre of the lower row, flanked on each side by a fierce animal, one of which is devouring a human figure. In the upper row are two goat-like creatures and a diaper ornament. This mixture of figural and geometrical motives is typical of early Anglo-Norman sculpture.

20. SOUTH MILTON (DEVON), ALL SAINTS' ; font. *Early twelfth*

Only the cup-shaped bowl is decorated with sculpture ; the base remains plain. The thick cable moulding divides the font into two. Plain triangles pointing upwards rest on the cable moulding and provide a rhythmical division of the bowl. Heads and foliage motives are carved between each triangle. Around the upper part of the bowl a continuous strip of sculpture includes amongst other figures a dancing girl and a bird. This font is frequently called crude or even savage. True enough, it is certainly a rustic work, but it is well composed and forceful. The motive of the dancing girl bending back to the ground and the head below her may have been inspired by representations of the Dance of Salome.

21. TOLLER FRATRUM (DORSET), ST. BASIL'S ; font. *First half of the twelfth century.*

This font is cylindrical, with its upper rim decorated with regular interlacements and cable band. The rim is supported by the raised arms of figures in relief. Other, smaller figures, or heads of figures only, and birds perched on columns, fill the remaining surface. There was here an evident anxiety not to leave any empty space. The motive of supporters familiar to us from the example in Durham Castle (Fig. 9), was frequent in Romanesque sculpture and it was often used with the object of giving plastic expression to the idea of weight and of its support. The slender rim of the Toller Fratrum font hardly needs any great support and the carvings here are purely decorative, beautifully balanced by the alternating use of the tall figures of the supporters, or other tall motives, with the tiny figures or heads of figures only placed between them.

22. FINCHAM (NORFOLK), ST. MARTIN'S ; font. *Early twelfth century.*
The scene represents the Adoration of the Magi, the subjects on the other sides of the square bowl of the font being the Nativity, the Baptism, and Adam and Eve. The growing interest of Anglo-Norman sculptors in religious subjects is shown here in the attempt to illustrate a biblical scene. But they still had a long way to go before finding a suitable treatment for such subjects. The Norfolk sculptor placed each Magi under a separate arch ; each figure is treated in an identical, doll-like manner, facing the spectator. These figures are expressionless, but they form part of a decorative scheme in which one motive is repeated several times as if it were an ornamental pattern : there is thus complete unity between the figures, the arcades, and the diaper ornament above and below them.

23. BREDWARDINE (HEREFORDSHIRE), ST. ANDREW'S ; lintel over the north doorway. *Early twelfth century.*
The lintel is inserted into a plain eleventh century doorway. The decoration of the lintel consists of geometrical patterns with two figures under arcades in the centre. The figures are damaged, so that certainty is difficult, but the scene may have been intended to represent the Temptation of Christ.

24. HANDBOROUGH (OXFORDSHIRE), ST. PETER'S ; tympanum over the north doorway. *Early twelfth century.*
The patron saint of the church with his keys occupies the centre of the tympanum, with the symbol of St. Mark to the left and the Agnus Dei to the right. The modelling of St. Peter is clumsy and the proportions of the figure are too short. For a long time the Anglo-Norman sculptors were much happier in their carving of animals, foliage or simply geometrical patterns, and it was only later in the period that really satisfying results in figure sculpture were achieved.

25-26. LONDON, VICTORIA AND ALBERT MUSEUM ; capital from Westminster Hall. *Between* 1090 *and* 1100.
The subject carved here represents an assault on a castle by a man with an axe and a shield ; he is shown in a strange attitude, as if kneeling. The castle stands on piers, and steep steps lead to its entrance : many castles are so depicted on the famous Bayeux Tapestry. This is one of the oldest " historiated " or narrative capitals in England.

27. HEREFORD CATHEDRAL ; capital from the choir. *Circa* 1115.
The series of " historiated " capitals at Hereford, one of which, the Harrowing of Hell, is illustrated here, are replaced by modern copies and are now lying loose in the church. Their style, heavy perhaps, but forceful and expressive, shows definite links with pre-Conquest Anglo-Saxon works, such as the panel with the Harrowing of Hell scene at Bristol (*circa* 1050).

28. HEREFORD CATHEDRAL ; capital from the choir. *Circa* 1115.

Another example of the Hereford series, Christ in Majesty, is particularly impressive in its simple, summary treatment of the figure and its forceful gesture.

29-30. SOUTHWELL MINSTER (NOTTINGHAMSHIRE) ; capitals of the crossing. *Circa* 1120.

These examples are among the most important series of " historiated " capitals in England. Decorated with New Testament scenes, they are characterised by a linear style based on the drawing technique of some illuminated manuscripts.

31. MORETON VALENCE (GLOUCESTERSHIRE), ST. STEPHEN'S ; tympanum over the north doorway. *Circa* 1120.

St. Michael fighting the dragon carved here is not conceived as a dramatic combat between good and evil : English sculptors of that period seldom attempted to depict strong emotions in religious subjects. Their aims were rather decorative ; they sought a harmonious balance of forms, soft modelling and a feeling of almost lyrical serenity. It is very instructive to compare the Gloucestershire tympanum with a tympanum with a similar subject in a French church (Saint-Michel d'Entraigues, Charente), carved some twenty years later (Fig. 32). Notice the violent movement of St. Michael on the French relief. He treads on the body of the dragon and thrusts his spear through the head of the monster while his cloak floats out behind him to convey the forward movement of the Saint. In comparison with all this the English carving is almost static : the Saint leans slightly forward, almost like a dancer, his spear just touches the monster's head and the cloak, instead of floating out behind, hangs down in front of the figure. Other details, such as the knot on the dragon's tail and the foliage, underline the decorative, almost ornamental, character of the English sculpture.

32. SAINT-MICHEL D'ENTRAIGUES (CHARENTE) ; tympanum. *Circa* 1140. (See Fig. 31.)

33. WINCHESTER CATHEDRAL ; corbels of the south transept. *Soon after* 1107.

The central tower of the church fell down in that year and damaged the south transept, which was, however, soon restored. It was then that this corbel-table was erected to crown the uppermost stretch of the exterior walls. Its form is very elaborate : the projecting wall is arched and supported by a series of grotesque corbels. The idea of the carved corbels came to England from the Continent and soon became one of the favourite features of English Romanesque architecture. The corbels of the Winchester series are not only amongst the earliest in England but are also amongst the wittiest.

34. CANTERBURY CATHEDRAL; exterior arcades of the choir. *Circa* 1120.

Christ Church, Canterbury, was not only the metropolitan church but also the largest Benedictine monastery in the country. It is not surprising, therefore, to find that its decoration was unrivalled at that time by anything else in England. In spite of subsequent fire and the extensive rebuilding of the choir, enough still remains of the early twelfth century decoration to support this view. The exterior arcading, composed of shafts, carved capitals with arches above them, plain and intersecting, runs around the whole length of the choir, its towers and transepts, as a highly decorative and unifying motive.

35. CANTERBURY CATHEDRAL; column in the crypt under the choir. *Circa* 1120.

While on the exterior of churches the sculpture was applied mainly to the doorways, to the corbel-tables and sometimes to the decorative arcades, inside the churches it was the capitals and sometimes the columns that provided the sculptor with his greatest opportunities. Of this, as of so much else, Canterbury Cathedral affords some of the finest examples.

36. HOOK NORTON (OXFORDSHIRE), ST. PETER'S; font. *First half of the twelfth century.*

Of the interior fittings of churches the altars, the shrines and the fonts are those that naturally received the most sumptuous decoration. But altars and shrines were usually made of precious materials, and so very few examples have come down to us; no English altar or shrine of that type survives. Fonts, however, were made of stone or lead and were of less material value. For this reason there are some hundreds of fonts of the twelfth century alone still existing in England, many of them quite elaborately carved. The subjects frequently relate to the sacrament of Baptism or to the Baptism of Christ. But even more often, perhaps, they are secular. The Hook Norton font with its mixture of religious and secular subjects, is a fairly typical example. The Adam and Eve subject is an obvious allusion to absolution from the Original Sin through baptism. Two signs of the Zodiac are placed next to them: Sagittarius and Aquarius for September and November respectively.

37. STEYNING (SUSSEX), ST. ANDREW'S; relief on a respond shaft of the south aisle. *Circa* 1120.

The shafts were often decorated with geometrical or foliage motives and also, occasionally, with figure sculpture. This is one of the earliest examples of the latter method.

38. WANSFORD (NORTHAMPTONSHIRE), ST. MARY'S; font. *Circa* 1120.

Fairly close stylistically to the Steyning relief (Fig. 37). It is decorated with the scene of the Baptism of Christ, figures of saints under a continuous arcade, and two warriors with clubs and shields, fighting. The font was a product of a regional school active in Northamptonshire in the first half of the twelfth century (see below).

39. CASTOR (NORTHAMPTONSHIRE), ST. KYNEBURGHA'S ; capitals of the tower arch. 1124.

The church at Castor is dated by a dedicatory inscription, a rare and valuable occurrence: the lack of precise dates is a serious obstacle in our study of the stylistic changes in twelfth century sculpture. One of the capitals at Castor is carved with a fruit-gathering scene. There are similar scenes in contemporary illuminated manuscripts, from which they probably found their way into the sculptors' sketch-books.

40. LONDON, BRITISH MUSEUM ; Cotton MS. Claudius E.V., folio 49. *First half of the twelfth century.*

This vigorous and amusing illumination representing a man gathering fruit and an animal playing the flute came from the scriptorium of Christ Church, Canterbury, which had a profound influence on contemporary sculpture (see Figs. 39 and 56).

41. CASTOR (NORTHAMPTONSHIRE), ST. KYNEBURGHA'S ; capital of the chancel arch. 1124.

While it is likely that the previously noted capital at Castor (Fig. 39) was inspired by contemporary illuminated manuscripts, this example, carved with a boar hunting scene (the man with a long spear carved on the side of the capital is not visible in our photograph) is probably imitated from a Roman relief of Meleager hunting the wild boar of Calydon. Roman sculpture was known to twelfth century English sculptors either directly (there were, no doubt, numerous Roman sculptures still in existence in England), or indirectly, through Roman-inspired sculptures in contemporary France and Italy.

42. CASTOR (NORTHAMPTONSHIRE), ST. KYNEBURGHA'S ; capital of the tower arch. 1124.

The use of a head at the angle of a capital to serve the purpose of the angle volute was one of the most popular motives in Romanesque sculpture. In England it was used for the first time in the crypt of Durham Castle (about 1072) but soon this motive developed into something entirely new. The size of the head increased and it was no longer confined to the upper part of the capital but spread along its whole length : in fact it replaced the capital. The change was not immediate. In intermediate examples, such as the capital here illustrated, there is still a little surface left on either side of the head, used in this case for ornamental foliage that issues from the nose of the head.

43-44. WEST HADDON (NORTHAMPTONSHIRE), ALL SAINTS'; font. *Circa* 1120.

This font although almost contemporary with the Castor capitals is not the work of the same school. Its close stylistic links with the "historiated" capitals at Southwell Minster (Figs. 29 and 30) suggest that it probably came from further north, from a workshop related to that at Southwell. The carvings on the font illustrate various episodes from the life of Christ. The scene of Christ's baptism, especially, has the charm and sincerity of a truly inspired work. Christ does not stand in the Jordan, as he is usually represented in that scene, but in a font with a beaded rim, exactly like the rim of the font that it decorates. On one side St. John the Baptist humbly approaches Christ; he holds a book and the other hand is upraised in benediction. On the other side an angel waits, holding Christ's cloak. At the angles, as if it were not a font but a capital, large heads are carved with foliage issuing from their mouths. The other scene illustrated here represents the Entry into Jerusalem.

45. LUPPITT (DEVON), ST. MARY'S; font. *First half of the twelfth century.*

The twelfth century witnessed the growth of various regional centres of stone sculpture. Some of these, although they cannot claim to be of the highest artistic importance, show a forceful and expressive style. The font at Luppitt belongs to the same artistic centre as the font at South Milton (Fig. 20) and is a further development of the same decorative if fierce style. The sculpture is modelled in rather high relief and the human and animal forms are further enriched with incised lines. The verticals and the horizontals of the composition are perfectly balanced, forming a logical pattern all round the bowl.

46. THORPE ARNOLD (LEICESTERSHIRE), ST. MARY MAGDALENE'S; font. *Early twelfth century.*

In comparison with the previous example it is the crude work of a village sculptor, yet it reveals a characteristic that is common to both: a fierce, almost savage element in the animal sculpture. The St. Michael scene on the Thorpe Arnold font is totally different from the same subject on the tympanum at Moreton Vallence (Fig. 31). At Moreton Vallence the scene is treated almost lyrically. The St. Michael scene at Thorpe Arnold sprang from very different traditions. The flat relief, the precise outlines and the fierceness of the animal forms recall the Scandinavian-derived art of pre-Conquest England.

47. CANTERBURY CATHEDRAL; capital in the crypt under the tower of St. Andrew. *Circa* 1120.

By far the most important regional school of sculpture of the Romanesque period in England was in the southern part of the country. It originated at Canterbury about 1120 under the strong influence of illuminated manuscripts as well as of such other sources as the Roman sculptures in England, oriental textiles, and ivories. The capital here illustrated is one of the most beautiful works of the school. It is carved with vigorous animal and foliage motives admirably fitted to the cushion shape of the capital.

48. ROMSEY ABBEY (HAMPSHIRE); capitals of the choir aisle. *Circa* 1140.

A further elaboration of the method applied to the previous example. The simple cushion shape has developed into the scalloped capital, with the increased number of semi-circles. Here the decorative qualities of the Southern School touched their heights.

49. CANTERBURY CATHEDRAL; capital in the main crypt. *Circa* 1120.

The carvings of the Canterbury crypt combine a brilliant technique with great inventiveness in the motives. Here, for instance, is a lion with huge tusks and a tail that ends in a leaf and berries.

50. CANTERBURY CATHEDRAL; capital in the main crypt. *Circa* 1120.

A bird devouring a snake-like creature. Combat between birds and snakes is common to both Persian and Hindu mythology and it was through the medium of oriental textiles, ivories or metalwork that this subject found its way to Canterbury.

51-52. CANTERBURY CATHEDRAL; capital in the main crypt. *Circa* 1120.

These are two sides of the same capital and the carved figures doubtless represent *jongleurs*. The *jongleurs* of the middle ages entertained with music, songs, poetry, dancing, and with tumbling and conjuring tricks. The Canterbury carvings depict some humorous performance by two men with a bowl and fish.

53. CANTERBURY CATHEDRAL; capital in the main crypt. *Circa* 1120.

This is the third side of the same capital. Here we have a very different subject: two fantastic, monstrous creatures—a two-headed female riding a composite monster, part bird, part fish, part quadruped. This vigorous composition, full of dynamic movement and fierce expression, is one of the masterpieces of English medieval sculpture.

54. CANTERBURY CATHEDRAL; capital in the main crypt. *Circa* 1120.

This is yet another, the fourth, side of the same capital and it shows the same mastery in rendering movement, and tremendous force.

55-56. CANTERBURY CATHEDRAL; capital in the crypt under the tower of St. Anselm. *Circa* 1120.

The subject of animals playing musical instruments was very popular in Romanesque art and was based on humorous fables. One of the most frequent scenes of this type shows a donkey playing the lyre. There are many examples in contemporary French and Italian sculpture of scenes depicting animals playing musical instruments, but in none of them is a complicated composition tackled with such ease as here, nor do they show such rich imagination nor such accomplished draughtmanship and modelling. The carving was inspired by local illuminated manuscripts. This can be seen by comparing the dog playing a flute on the capital (Fig. 56) with a similar motive in a Canterbury illumination (Fig. 40).

57. CANTERBURY CATHEDRAL ; capital in the main crypt. *Circa* 1120.

This is a highly decorative and vigorous treatment of the motive already seen and commented on at Castor (Fig. 42).

58. CANTERBURY, MUSEUM OF ST. AUGUSTINE'S COLLEGE ; corbel from St. Augustine's Abbey. *Circa* 1120.

The few extant fragments of sculpture from St. Augustine's Abbey make it clear that the sculptors who so brilliantly decorated the cathedral were also employed in the decoration of the second large Benedictine monastery in Canterbury. The name of one of them is revealed to us by an inscription on this corbel "ROBERTUS ME FECIT." The corbel is much more elaborate than those at Winchester (Fig. 33): it represents a man holding two dogs by their tails while they bite his beard.

59. READING MUSEUM ; capital from Reading Abbey. *Circa* 1130.

Reading Abbey was a foundation of Henry I begun in 1121. To-day only a few sad ruins of that great abbey remain. A certain amount of its sculptural decoration has been found in Reading and its neighbourhood, in rockery gardens, ornamental arches, or used simply as building material. This capital was part of the original cloister arcade and it shows a great stylistic indebtedness to Canterbury. Compare, for instance, the Reading capital with the capital in the crypt at Canterbury: a monster fighting a dog (Fig. 54). The composition of the Reading sculpture is strictly symmetrical: two S-shaped creatures biting their own legs. But the violent movement and the modelling is strikingly similar.

60. DURHAM CATHEDRAL ; capitals of the inside face of the north doorway. *Circa* 1130.

The exquisite sculpture decorating this doorway is strongly linked with local illuminated manuscripts and is perhaps not unconnected with the Southern School. But the cushion shape of the capitals so strongly emphasised by the sculpture in so

35

many examples of the Southern School, at Canterbury (Fig. 47), Romsey (Fig. 48) and elsewhere, is here completely disregarded, and the sculpture spreads deliberately over the whole surface with equal emphasis.

61. READING MUSEUM; capital from Reading Abbey. *Circa* 1130.
The figure sculpture of the early Romanesque period was either grotesque, as at Canterbury (Figs. 50 and 51) or purely decorative as in this example from Reading. Two seated figures of saints, one giving the blessing and the other with a pastoral staff and probably therefore an abbot (St. Benedict?) form part of a composition that is quite unorthodox. First, they are placed within the mandorlas, the signs of glory reserved only for Christ but here used merely as frames for the figures; secondly, they have the wings of angels, but, as the staff indicates, they are not angels. Moreover, these wings are attached to the nimbuses for a purely decoratiive reason: to form two semi-circles, a motive suggested to the sculptor by the scallop-shaped capitals. The treatment of the hair and particularly that of the folds of the robes, marked by parallel grooves, is decorative and without any relation to the shapes of the bodies underneath. The result achieved is a composition of great ornamental richness.

62. LONDON, VICTORIA AND ALBERT MUSEUM; capital from Reading Abbey. *Circa* 1130.
For two reasons this is a very notable sculpture. It is clear that the intention here is far more realistic than in the previous example. There is some effort to render truthfully the movements and gestures, and the proportions, of the figures and to express emotions. The second notable feature of the sculpture is its subject. It represents the Coronation of the Virgin, the subject thought till recently to be the invention of French Gothic art. This English example is the oldest known representation of that scene.

63. READING MUSEUM; capital from Reading Abbey. *Circa* 1130.
Sculpture within medallions or rings was one of the favourite motives of the Southern School. In this case two medallions decorate each side of the capital and are joined in pairs by decorative masks. Within the medallions animal and foliage motives are admirably fitted into the circular fields.

64 and 66. ST. MARYCHURCH (DEVON); font. *Second quarter of the twelfth century.*
Sculpture contained within medallions was equally popular outside the Southern School. This font, for instance, has a chain of seven medallions with reliefs representing a harpist, a dancing girl, a hunter blowing his horn, a boar attacked by a dog (Fig. 64), another hunter on horseback pursuing an animal and a bird (Fig. 66).

65. WINCHESTER, ST. BARTHOLOMEW'S; capital from Hyde Abbey. *Circa* 1130.

Winchester was one of the centres of the Southern School in close relation with Canterbury and Reading. Several of the capitals surviving from Hyde Abbey are, like those at Reading, decorated with medallions containing animals and foliage. But the Winchester capitals have only single medallions on each side.

66. *See* Fig. 64.

67. LONDON, VICTORIA AND ALBERT MUSEUM; relief from the cloister of Reading Abbey. *Circa* 1130.

This sculpture was perhaps intended to represent " the Pelican in her Piety." In that scene the bird pecks its own breast to feed its young with its own blood; the symbol of Christ's sacrifice. If the Reading relief was intended to be the pelican it was, nevertheless, used more as a decorative motive, part of an interlacement, than as the symbolical subject. In spite of its damaged condition, the very delicate treatment of the details of the sculpture is still evident.

68. ROMSEY ABBEY; capital in the north choir aisle. *Circa* 1140.

In contrast to the previous example, in which the bird was treated as an integral part of an interlacing pattern, this capital representing an owl goes a step further towards independent, three-dimensional figure sculpture.

69. CHARNEY BASSET (BERKSHIRE), ST. PETER'S; tympanum representing " Alexander's Ascent." *Second quarter of the twelfth century.*

The legend of the celestial journey of Alexander the Great carried by griffins was extremely popular throughout the middle ages and was represented in numerous sculptures. The Charney Basset tympanum lacks some of the usual details, e.g. the King's bait on two sticks, but otherwise the composition is clearly based on the legend. Stylistically this sculpture shows some influence of Reading, quite natural in view of the nearness of that important centre of the Southern School.

70. ROCHESTER CATHEDRAL; detail of the doorway to the chapter house. *Circa* 1140.

There is a great deal in common between the decoration of this doorway and the earlier works of the Southern School, at Canterbury, for instance. The sculpture here, however, is more plastic: observe the heads carved in full relief. This tendency towards higher relief announces a further period in the development of English Romanesque sculpture.

71. LONDON, BRITISH MUSEUM; capital from Lewes Priory (Sussex). *Circa* 1140.

This new tendency towards three-dimensional sculpture is well illustrated by this example, representing the miraculous draught of fishes. As a result of giving his figures a high relief and cutting away the background to a considerable depth the sculptor found some difficulty in joining the reliefs on different sides of the capital: at the angles where the various reliefs meet there is a certain awkwardness resulting from this deep under cutting of the figures.

72. LEWES MUSEUM; capital from Lewes Priory. *Circa* 1140.
This is undoubtedly the work of the sculptor who carved the previous example. Here, however, he overcame the difficulty of joining the reliefs on the four sides of the capital by a repetition of the motive of a bird carved within concentric medallions.

73-74. WINCHESTER CATHEDRAL; capital. *Circa* 1140.
With such works as this capital the early, " decorative " period of Romanesque sculpture in England ends. The development from linear into plastic sculpture is complete. The centaur fighting a sea monster, and another killing a griffin, are treated here not as ornamental patterns but as sculptures in the round.

75. WINCHESTER CITY MUSEUM; capital. *Circa* 1140.
The sculpture represents eight figures of ecclesiastics seated under arcades. Each figure holds a book and raises his hand in benediction. The majestic gravity of the figures, the logical modelling of their bodies, the composition of the rhythmically repeated arcades, create a work of art of the first order. It is probably contemporary with the previous capital and it also shows that the decorative style of the early twelfth century was replaced towards the middle of the century by a plastic and more monumental style.

76. NORWICH CATHEDRAL; capital, probably from the cloister. *Circa* 1140.
The development towards a more sculptural form is not common to all the English work of the second quarter of the twelfth century. Indeed, some works dating from even the second half still exhibit the linear style more characteristic of the beginning of the century. This linear style had a particularly strong and lasting tradition in East Anglia. The flat, abstract sculpture of the Viking conquerors was still remembered and imitated. This Norwich capital, carved with two snake-like dragons interlacing with foliage, has the same quality of abstract geometrical interlacements, in which the zoomorfic forms are almost entirely lost, as the Viking metal-works and wood sculptures.

77-78. ELY CATHEDRAL; Priors' Doorway. *Circa* 1140.
The linear style so typical of some Norwich capitals is found in the decoration of this wonderful doorway at Ely. Although it is possible to trace a great many foreign elements in the sculpture of the tympanum, or of the door jambs, and even in

the general design of the doorway and in the method of the application of sculpture to it, the basic style is typically English, with that peculiar mixture of different elements that one could meet nowhere but on English soil.

79. NORWICH CATHEDRAL; capital, probably from the cloister. *Circa* 1140.

Although this example is much more Romanesque than the other capital illustrated here (Fig. 76), it, too, has that linear quality that brings to one's mind the openwork metal ornaments of the Vikings. The large trefoiled leaves are, however, characteristic of the second quarter of the twelfth century. The style of the carving is so closely related to the decoration of Ely (Fig. 78) that we can, with some probability, talk of an East Anglian workshop, responsible for the decoration of both Ely and Norwich.

80-82. CHICHESTER CATHEDRAL; two reliefs in the choir. *Circa* 1140.

The reliefs depict the story of the raising of Lazarus. They are over three feet square and consist of numerous pieces of stone joined together. Originally they probably formed part of a screen. The first relief represents " Christ at Mary's house " and the second the " Raising of Lazarus." Both panels were found, re-used as building material, behind the stalls of the cathedral in the middle of the nineteenth century. Yet, except for minor injuries the sculptures are in a good state of preservation, although all the eyes of the figures, which were originally inlaid with lead or glass paste, are now empty cavities. The date of these panels has been greatly disputed, some scholars claiming for them a date as early as about 1000. And without doubt there are elements in these panels derived from the sculpture of the pre-Conquest period. There are, however, certain analogies between the Chichester sculptures and the illuminations of the celebrated St. Albans Psalter that make it doubtful whether the panels can be dated before the execution of this manuscript, between 1119 and 1145. The great difficulty in dating the panels with any certainty is their very exceptional individual character. Both panels are probably the work of the same sculptor, although they differ greatly in dramatic expression. In the first, in which the two sisters meet Christ, the figures are solemn and dignified and the attention is concentrated on Christ, who occupies the centre of the composition and is the tallest of all the figures. In the second panel the figures express the tense drama of Lazarus' resurrection in a masterly fashion. The wig-like hair and beards and the theatrical gestures suggest that the sculptor of the Chichester panels was inspired by some contemporary mystery play. With these wonderful sculptures we are no longer in the early Romanesque period: in this art which mastered technique to give expression to an intense religious faith we enter the period of maturity.

SUGGESTIONS FOR FURTHER READING

F. BOND, *Fonts and Font Covers*, London, New York, Toronto, 1908.

A. W. CLAPHAM, *English Romanesque Architecture after the Conquest*, Oxford, 1934.

A. GARDNER, *A Handbook of English Medieval Sculpture*, Cambridge, 1935.

T. D. KENDRICK, *Late Saxon and Viking Art*, London, 1949.

C. E. KEYSER, *A List of Norman Tympana and Lintels*, London, Second Edition, 1927.

D. KNOWLES, *The Monastic Order in England*, Cambridge, 1949.

E. S. PRIOR & A. GARDNER, *An Account of Medieval Figure-Sculpture in England*, Cambridge, 1912.

ACKNOWLEDGEMENTS

The writer wishes to thank the following for permission to reproduce photographs: Mr. F. H. Crossley (Figs. 60, 77 and 80-82); the National Buildings Record (Figs. 2, 15, 20-22, 29-31, 36, 45, 46, 64, 66, 69, 76 and 79); the Royal Commission on Historical Monuments (Fig. 58); The Warburg Institute (Figs. 1, 3, 5-9, 75). He is also indebted to his colleagues at the Courtauld Institute of Art for their invaluable help in the preparation of the illustrations. Finally he wishes to thank Mr. J. L. Frith for reading the manuscript.

1. DURHAM CASTLE CHAPEL. *Circa* 1072.

2. ST. JOHN'S CHAPEL, TOWER OF LONDON. *Circa* 1080.

3. DURHAM CASTLE CHAPEL—capital. *Circa* 1072.

4. GLOUCESTER CATHEDRAL—capital in the crypt. *Circa* 1089.

5.　DURHAM CASTLE CHAPEL—capital.　*Circa* 1072.

6.　DURHAM CASTLE CHAPEL—capital.　*Circa* 1072.

7. DURHAM CASTLE CHAPEL—capital. *Circa* 1072.

8. DURHAM CASTLE CHAPEL—capital. *Circa* 1072.

9. DURHAM CASTLE CHAPEL—capital. *Circa* 1072.

10. DIJON, SAINT-BENIGNE—capital in the crypt. *Early 11th century.*

11. CANTERBURY CATHEDRAL—capital in the crypt. *Circa* 1075.

12. BRAMBER (SUSSEX), ST. NICHOLAS'—capital of the chancel arch.
Late 11*th century.*

13. NEWTON IN CLEVELAND (YORKSHIRE, NORTH RIDING),
ST. OSWALD'S—carved stone. *Late 11th century.*

14. DIJON, SAINT-BENIGNE—capital in the crypt. *Early 11th century.*

15. UPPINGTON (SHROPSHIRE). HOLY TRINITY—tympanum over the
north doorway. *Late 11th century.*

16. BYTON (HEREFORDSHIRE), ST. MARY'S—tympanum built into the south wall. *Early 12th century.*

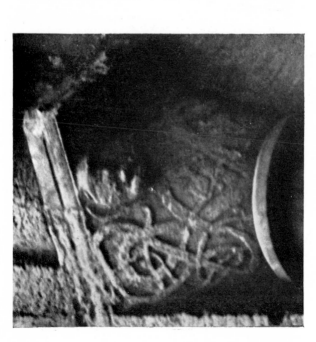

17 - 18. KIRKBURN (YORKSHIRE). ST. MARY'S—capital of the nave window. *Circa* 1100.

19. BARTON SEAGRAVE (NORTHAMPTONSHIRE), ST. BOTOLPH'S—tympanum over the north doorway. *Circa* 1100.

20. SOUTH MILTON (DEVON). ALL SAINTS'.—font.
Early 12th century.

21. TOLLER FRATRUM (DORSET). ST. BASIL'S.—font.
First half of the 12th century.

22. FINCHAM (NORFOLK), ST. MARTIN'S—font. *Early 12th century.*

23. BREDWARDINE (HEREFORDSHIRE). ST. ANDREW'S—lintel over the north doorway. *Early 12th century*

24. HANDBOROUGH (OXFORDSHIRE), ST. PETER'S—tympanum over the north doorway. *Early 12th century.*

25 - 26. LONDON, VICTORIA AND ALBERT MUSEUM—capital from
Westminster Hall. *Between* 1090 - 1100.

27. HEREFORD CATHEDRAL—capital from the choir. *Circa* 1115.

28. HEREFORD CATHEDRAL—capital from the choir. *Circa* 1115.

29 - 30. SOUTHWELL MINSTER (NOTTINGHAMSHIRE)—capitals of the crossing. *Circa* 1120.

31. MORETON VALENCE (GLOUCESTERSHIRE), ST. STEPHEN'S—
tympanum over the north doorway. *Circa* 1120.

32. SAINT-MICHEL D'ENTRAIGUES (CHARENTE)—tympanum.
Circa 1140.

33. WINCHESTER CATHEDRAL—corbels of the south transept. *Soon after* 1107.

34. CANTERBURY CATHEDRAL—exterior arcades of the choir. *Circa* 1120.

35. CANTERBURY CATHEDRAL—column in the crypt under the choir.
Circa 1120.

56. HOOK NORTON (OXFORDSHIRE), ST. PETER'S—font.
First half of the 12th century.

37 STEYNING (SUSSEX). ST ANDREW'S, relief on a reused shaft

38. WANSFORD (NORTHAMPTONSHIRE), ST. MARY'S—font. *Circa* 1120.

39. CASTOR (NORTHAMPTONSHIRE), ST. KYNEBURGHA'S—
capitals of the tower arch. 1124.

40. LONDON, BRITISH MUSEUM—Cotton MS. Claudius E.V., folio 49.
First half of the 12th century.

41. CASTOR (NORTHAMPTONSHIRE), ST. KYNEBURGHA'S—capital of the chancel arch. 1124.

42. CASTOR (NORTHAMPTONSHIRE), ST. KYNEBURGHA'S—capital of the tower arch. 1124.

43 - 44. WEST HADDON (NORTHAMPTONSHIRE), ALL SAINTS'—font. *Circa* 1120.

45. LUPPITT (DEVON), ST. MARY's—font. *First half of the 12th century.*

46. THORPE ARNOLD (LEICESTERSHIRE), ST. MARY MAGDALENE'S—font.
Early 12th century.

47. CANTERBURY CATHEDRAL—capital in the crypt under the tower of St. Andrew. *Circa* 1120.

48. ROMSEY ABBEY (HAMPSHIRE)—capitals of the choir aisle. *Circa* 1140.

49. CANTERBURY CATHEDRAL—capital in the main crypt. *Circa* 1120.

50. CANTERBURY CATHEDRAL—capital in the main crypt. *Circa* 1120.

51 - 52. CANTERBURY CATHEDRAL—capital in the main crypt. *Circa* 1120.

53. CANTERBURY CATHEDRAL—capital in the main crypt. *Circa* 1120.

54. CANTERBURY CATHEDRAL—capital in the main crypt. *Circa* 1120.

55 - 56. CANTERBURY CATHEDRAL—capital in the crypt under the tower of St. Anselm. *Circa* 1120.

57. CANTERBURY CATHEDRAL—capital in the main crypt. *Circa* 1120.

58. CANTERBURY, MUSEUM OF ST. AUGUSTINE'S COLLEGE—corbel from St. Augustine's Abbey. *Circa* 1120.

59. READING MUSEUM—capital from Reading Abbey. *Circa* 1130.

60. DURHAM CATHEDRAL—capitals of the inside face of the north
doorway. *Circa* 1130.

61. READING MUSEUM—capital from Reading Abbey. *Circa* 1130.

62. London, Victoria and Albert Museum—capital from Reading Abbey. *Circa* 1130.

63. Reading Museum—capital from Reading Abbey. *Circa* 1130.

64. St. Marychurch (Devon)—font. *Second quarter of the 12th century.*

65. WINCHESTER, ST. BARTHOLOMEW'S—capital from Hyde Abbey. *C.* 1130.

66. ST. MARYCHURCH (DEVON)—font. *Second quarter of the 12th century.*

67. LONDON, VICTORIA AND ALBERT MUSEUM—relief from the cloister of Reading Abbey. *Circa* 1130.

68. ROMSEY ABBEY—capital in the north choir aisle. *Circa* 1140.

69. CHARNEY BASSET (BERKSHIRE) ST. PETER'S—tympanum representing "Alexander's Ascent."
Second quarter of the 12th century.

70. ROCHESTER CATHEDRAL—detail of the doorway to the chapter house. *Circa* 1140.

71. LONDON, BRITISH MUSEUM—capital from Lewes Priory (Sussex). *Circa* 1140.

72. LEWES MUSEUM—capital from Lewes Priory. *Circa* 1140.

73 - 74. WINCHESTER CATHEDRAL—capital. *Circa* 1140.

75. WINCHESTER CITY MUSEUM—capital. *Circa* 1140.

76. NORWICH CATHEDRAL—capital, probably from the cloister. *Circa* 1140.

77 ELY CATHEDRAL—Priors' Doorway. *Circa* 1140.

78. *Detail of figure 77.*

79. NORWICH CATHEDRAL—capital, probably from the cloister.
Circa 1140.

80 - 81.   CHICHESTER CATHEDRAL—two reliefs in the choir.
Circa 1140.

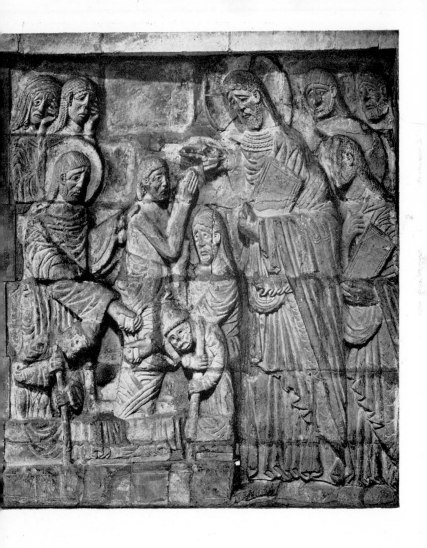

82. *Detail of figure 81.*